Welcome

Welcome

Thank you for opening this booklet.

This confidential space is for all of us who have been touched by miscarriage, whether the experience happened recently or years ago. Here you can reflect on what's happened and move through a healing process at your own pace.

Although you may feel isolated... you are not alone.

About one in four pregnancies ends in miscarriage.

Men, women, family members, and friends are all impacted by these losses.

Although miscarriage has touched many of us, we rarely talk about our experience.

Sometimes we lack the words to discuss the emotions that trouble us.

Other times we reach out only to have our grief minimized or ignored.

Sometimes we feel shame or guilt which only deepens our sense of isolation.

Wherever you are at, we hope this booklet will assist you as you grieve the loss of your child.

We invite you to start by reading and reflecting on the following stories shared by people who have experienced miscarriage – either their own or a loved one's.

There is hope after loss.

The stories in this booklet are real but individual's names have been changed to protect their identity, and the identity of their families, as they continue on their healing journeys.

Stories

"I always wanted to be a mom"

SARAH

I always wanted to be a mom.

I wanted lots and lots of kids.

I knew I would enjoy being pregnant… and I did.

Even morning sickness couldn't bring me down.

I knew it was all worth it.

When the nurse said, "I can't find a heartbeat,"

    I thought – keep looking. You'll find it. I feel it.

        Then the doctor said, "You've lost the baby."

And I thought, this cannot be happening.

But it happened.

And it hurt.

A lot.

It still does.

I never got to hold him.

I never got to tell him how much I loved him.

    I hope he knows.

        I want him to know I will never forget.

"I experienced my losses alone"
LUCIA

I experienced my first eight pregnancy losses alone.

Though I was married, my husband barely acknowledged the miscarriages. His brother died when he was young and I think the miscarriages brought up some old wounds that had never fully healed. I understood, and – in different ways – we were each alone.

After 23 years of marriage and the birth of two children, my husband and I divorced.

After a few years, I became romantically involved with a friend who had been a huge emotional support.

When I learned that we were expecting, I let myself envision raising a family with a man I adored and respected.

> But almost immediately, my inner knowing told me that the pregnancy wasn't viable.

> Eight weeks later, I had a miscarriage.

During those eight weeks, I wanted to tell my friend. But he was under extraordinary strain at the time and I didn't have the heart to cause him more stress.

> Months later, when his stress had eased, I told him about the baby. I apologized for not sharing the news earlier and explained that I would have done so if I had thought there was even a slight chance that the pregnancy was viable.

Since I wasn't sure that I had made the best decision, I asked him to trust my intentions and to find it in his heart to forgive me.

He wasn't angry, and he understood why I hadn't told him.

He said one thing about the baby which was the kindest response I could have anticipated, "I would have been a very lucky man."

I will forever be grateful that during such a painful time he was able to respond with such graciousness and with a kindness that helped heal my heart.

"No one asked about me"

DARRIL

Sometimes I think I am the only one that remembers the day –
the day my wife miscarried our first child.

Doctors told me how to take care of her – physically.

Her mother told me to take her home, tuck her in bed, and
not to be surprised if she woke in the middle of the night
crying – she did.

Her sister came over the next day to sit with her.

Friends brought over dinner.

    To this day, I am not sure anyone ever asked about me.

      I woke up in the middle of the night crying too.

        I keep the hospital bracelet from that day
        tucked away in a secret place.

Every year I take it out, look at it, hold it in my hand, and
remember our first child.

    I wonder how our family would have been different.

      I still miss him.

"I wish I could do more"

JADA

I was pregnant when my sister suffered her second miscarriage.

I felt awful.

I was afraid I would make her feel even worse.

I even told our mother, "I'm the last person she will want to see."

But I went to visit anyway. I told her I was so sorry.

Mostly, we talked about how our babies would have loved each other – the fun they would have had together – the messes they would have made – the joys we would have shared. At other times, we sat in silence. I didn't know what else to say.

I know my sister still misses her baby.

I miss him too.

I know sometimes she looks at my son and wonders what might have been. I do too.

I wish I could do more...

"I was sad too"

MARIA

Some days you never forget.

I was with my daughter. She was 12 weeks pregnant. The doctor said she miscarried and then they said it would be okay. She could try again.

But she wasn't okay. Neither was I.

For a long time, all she could do was talk about what might have been.

All I could do was listen.

But I was sad too.

I still am.

It is hard to watch your child suffer. To not know what to do or say. You just do the best you can.

I still miss her baby – my grandchild. I know she does too, but we don't talk about it very much anymore.

I know he or she would have looked like my daughter

– laughed like her

– loved like her.

I think of our grandchild every year on that day.

I think of what life would have been like – the fun we would have had.

We just didn't get the chance.

"We'd been trying for a long time"
SOPHIA

We'd been trying to add to our family for a long time.

Finally, I saw the Plus Sign.

I was excited – relieved – scared.

I told my husband… he was elated.

We relished in the secret for a week and then couldn't wait any longer to share the news.

Then at six weeks I started to bleed.

The doctor told us, "It's normal."

The nurse told us, "It's not your fault."

I replayed their words over and over… but it didn't help.

People told me I was lucky it happened so fast.

I didn't feel lucky.

I felt betrayed – lost – lonely.

Healing Pathways

Healing Pathways

Miscarriage hurts.

You are not alone.

Many

women

men

grandparents

siblings

and friends

are seeking to make sense of their own or their loved one's miscarriage.

This booklet is a safe place to begin.

Please use these pages to

tell your story

build support

explore emotions

identify losses

recognize unhealthy behaviors

and begin healing.

This space is yours.

Although the following sections suggest a healing pathway, the process isn't a set of orderly steps or stages.

Grief can intensify or diminish over time.

Sometimes you will feel fine... but then re-experience difficult emotions because of a specific event or perhaps for no reason at all.

Grieving and healing often feel messy and unpredictable.

Keep in mind that each person grieves differently – there is no set path or timeline.

Please remember there is always hope.

We invite you to turn the page and begin your journey.

Important Note: This booklet is not meant to take the place of professional counseling. Sometimes a miscarriage can create emotions that you may feel unequipped to deal with on your own.

If you have access to the Internet, please log on to MiscarriageHurts.com and use the Find Help Directory or Recognize Unhealthy Behaviors links to access national and local support resources. If you don't have access to the Internet, please call 2-1-1 and ask for assistance locating professional therapists, pregnancy loss support groups, or church counseling programs in your area. Call the National Suicide Prevention Lifeline at 1-800-273 TALK (8255) if you're thinking about or planning to hurt yourself.

Tell Your Story

Tell Your Story

Telling your story is important.

It will help you start or continue grieving the loss of your child or the child of someone close to you.

Telling your story will help you

       make sense of the experience

           connect with others

               and honor the one you lost.

It may be difficult or even painful to tell your story.

Keep in mind that you might need to make several attempts to start or finish it.

       That's okay.

Telling your story may stir up powerful emotions,

       or you may feel no emotion at all.

There is no right or wrong way to go about it.

The important thing is to acknowledge that your experience is real and that it is significant.

Included here are some questions that may help you tell your story – whether you have lost a child through miscarriage or are close to someone who has.

Questions to Consider If You Experienced a Miscarriage

<u>Before</u>

When did you find out you or your partner were pregnant?
How did you feel?
Whom did you tell?
What was their reaction?
Did you begin making plans for the child's arrival?

<u>During</u>

When did you suspect you or your partner were miscarrying the baby?
How did you feel?
Who accompanied you to the doctor's office or emergency room?
What happened there?
Were the medical personnel supportive?
Were you provided with information and referrals about remembrance services, support groups, and emotional support?

<u>After</u>

What happened right after the miscarriage?
Were you able to talk about it? If so, with whom?
What happened in the days and weeks that followed?
What happened in the months and years that followed?
What did you feel immediately afterward?
What do you feel now?
How has the miscarriage impacted your life?

Questions to Consider If Someone Close to You Experienced a Miscarriage

<u>Before</u>

When did you find out about the pregnancy?
What was your reaction?
What was her/his reaction?
Who else knew?
What role did you play, if any, as the pregnancy progressed?

<u>During</u>

When and where did the miscarriage take place?
Did you accompany her/him to the doctor's office or emergency room?
What was that like?
How did you feel?

<u>After</u>

What happened right after the miscarriage?
Were you able to talk about it? If so, with whom?
What happened in the days and weeks that followed?
What happened in the months and years that followed?
What did you feel immediately afterward?
What do you feel now?
How has the miscarriage impacted your life?

Use this space to tell your story – or if you want to anonymously share your story with others, you can submit it by visiting MiscarriageHurts.com/healing-pathways/tell-your-story.

Build Support

Build Support

As you reflect on your miscarriage, it will be helpful to reach out to others for support.

Telling your story to a trusted person and receiving support is so important.

> You do not need to make this journey alone.

Building a support system will require you to reveal your loss to at least one person:

> family member, friend, spiritual counselor, peer counselor, support group, or professional therapist.

Perhaps people close to you already know about the miscarriage and they didn't know what to say or do.

> Don't give up.

They probably didn't know how to support you or were afraid of hurting you – or it may have brought up painful emotions around a past loss.

When you are ready, gently let them know how they can help you or choose someone else to share your experience.

Think of a few people who might be able to support you. Use the space below to add their names.

Ask yourself these questions to see if they can provide the support you need.

Listening

Is this person a good listener?

Does this person automatically offer his or her opinion or advice?

Will this person try to minimize the loss or suggest it is insignificant in any way?

Does this person always seem busy or have a busy schedule?

Honesty

Will this person be honest with you if he or she doesn't have the resources to be the support you need?

Will this person support you in finding other resources, such as support groups or professional resources, if he or she thinks this is in your best interest?

Involvement

Has this person experienced a miscarriage in the past?

> *Keep in mind that some family members or friends may be experiencing troubling emotions or unresolved feelings about a past miscarriage. If that is the case, it may be best to seek someone else to be a part of your support system.*

Confidentiality

Will this person protect my confidentiality?

Has this person ever shared confidential information that I've told him or her in the past?

After reviewing the questions, you may want to remove some people from the previous list, and you may want to add others in the space provided below.

Get Started

As a concrete step, we encourage you to contact at least one person from your list today and set up a time to talk.

> Building your support system is important – it may take some time and effort.

But before long, you will find a person or two who will walk this journey with you.

> You are not alone!

To help prepare you, we've included some information about possible reactions you may encounter as you share your story.

Possible Reactions from Family Members or Friends

When you reveal a miscarriage, a person's initial reaction may not be what you'd hoped or expected.

If the pregnancy and/or miscarriage was a secret, then the person may be shocked, hurt, or even upset that you hadn't told them.

If the person knew about the miscarriage, then he or she may be surprised to learn it's still affecting you.

> Don't take their reaction – or lack of reaction – personally.

Because miscarriage is rarely talked about, it's normal for people to be confused about what to do or say.

However, in most cases the person will overcome their initial awkwardness and support you. You can help the members of your support system overcome their discomfort by sharing some specific ways they can help you, such as:

> Listening to your story.

> Calling you periodically just to see how you're doing.

> Helping you locate a professional therapist or support group if needed.

You may also want to refer them to the website MiscarriageHurts.com for more information.

Explore Emotions

Explore Emotions

Exploring your feelings is an important part of working through your miscarriage.

Denying, repressing, or pushing down emotions may work for a while,

> but at some point, you'll need to process your emotions in a safe environment.

> *Refusal to face these emotions can lead to unhealthy behaviors.*

People experience a variety of emotions at different times and at different levels of intensity.

This may be due to a number of factors, including age, gender, cultural influences, and past experiences.

You may already be in touch with your emotions,

> you may be numb to your emotions, or

> > you may be overwhelmed by your emotions.

Emotions may increase at particular times, such as around the time of significant dates or with certain reminders of the experience.

You may also find that you have different feelings regarding the same event or that some feelings reoccur over time.

> You may even experience mixed emotions such as relief and sadness at the same time.

Wherever you're at, this space is for you to either start or continue to explore the emotions associated with your miscarriage.

Exploring your emotions takes work – it can be painful and draining.

Although you may wish to do some of the work on your own, you'll benefit from communicating with your support system throughout the process.

> *If you find yourself becoming overwhelmed by your emotions, please seek help. Talk with your support system or use the Find Help Directory or Unhealthy Behaviors page in Healing Pathways on MiscarriageHurts.com to access local and national support resources.*

Identify Your Emotions

This exercise can help you begin to explore your feelings by first putting a name to them.

Read through the list of possible emotions and choose the ones that best describe how you feel.

You may choose emotions that you've felt at different times before, during, and after your loss, or you may simply want to choose emotions that you're feeling right now or have felt in the past several days or weeks.

Afraid	Forgiven	Isolated	Selfish
Alive	Forgotten	Jealous	Shocked
Alone	Fragile	Joyful	Sick
Angry	Free	Maternal	Spiritual
Anxious	Frozen	Miserable	Struggling
Ashamed	Frustrated	Mourning	Stuck
Betrayed	Grateful	Naked	Supported
Bleeding	Grieving	Needy	Sympathetic
Brave	Guilty	Neglected	Thoughtful
Broken	Happy	Numb	Threatened

Calm	Haunted	Nurtured	Tortured
Capable	Healing	Obsessed	Ugly
Changed	Healthy	Optimistic	Understood
Cleansed	Heartbroken	Overwhelmed	Unloved
Comforted	Helpless	Peaceful	Unprepared
Confused	Hopeful	Punished	Unworthy
Dead	Hopeless	Questioning	Uplifted
Degraded	Hypocritical	Rage	Used
Depressed	Impatient	Raped	Validated
Determined	Invisible	Raw	Valued
Dirty	Irrational	Ready	Violated
Discouraged	Longing	Relieved	Violent
Empowered	Lost	Renewed	Vulnerable
Empty	Loved	Resentful	Weak
Encouraged	Isolated	Ruined	Welcomed
Exhausted	Jealous	Sad	Worthless
Fake	Joyful	Safe	Wounded

If you're having trouble naming your emotions, don't get discouraged.

> If you've gotten in the habit of pushing down your emotions, it may take a while for you to start feeling them again.

It may help you to talk to members of your support system and request their feedback. Or, if you've written your story, refer back to it as it may contain emotions you felt before, during, or after the miscarriage.

People process emotions differently.

Be patient,

> give yourself time,

> > and remember that you are not alone.

If you're unable to get in touch with your emotions it may help to try something different like exploring your emotions via art, journaling, or poetry. When you have the time, review the creative activities below and see if one might work for you.

Explore Art

Explore your feelings through art. Feel free to explore whatever comes to mind or is in your heart.

Connecting with your feelings is an important part of healing.

Describing your emotions through drawing, painting, sculpture, collage, photography, and more may help you to process your loss(es) and the impact it's had on you and on others in your life.

Write a Poem

Describing your emotions through poetry may help you to process your loss(es) and the impact it's had on you and on others in your life.

Create a Journal Entry

Your journal should be a private space just for you.

Describing your emotions may help you process your loss(es) and the impact it's had on you and on others in your life.

Possible Journal Topics

Personal impact	Impact on others
Feelings	Loss(es)
Grieving	Unhealthy behaviors
Hope	Healing process
Random reflections	Remembering my child

This space is yours to explore feelings related to your miscarriage(s).

Identify Losses

Identify Losses

In the process of telling your story and exploring your emotions, you may have already identified losses that resulted from your miscarriage. Although this is a difficult step, you may feel a certain amount of relief when you're able to put a name to the losses you've experienced.

Examples of some losses you may feel:

- Loss of child, grandchild, brother or sister, niece or nephew

- Lost dreams for the child

- Lost opportunity to parent or grandparent

- Lost or weakened relationship with parents, family members, or friends

- Spiritual loss – feeling far away from or angry with God

- Loss of relationship with your partner

- Loss of self-esteem

- Loss of dreams, goals, or vision for your life

You can use the space below to identify your losses.

The losses you have experienced or are experiencing are real.

Identifying and acknowledging these losses is an important step toward healing.

Minimizing or denying them will not only impede the healing process, but it may also lead to unhealthy behaviors.

Deciding to accept and resolve them is important – it is a decision to grieve them and to feel pain.

Your losses are real.

Your grief is real.

Your pain is real.

Your ability to move through the grieving process and experience healing is also real.

Grief rarely moves through a series of steps in a linear fashion. It tends to intensify and diminish in cycles over a period of time. People work through their grief differently – some more quickly than others. The intensity of feelings also varies from person to person.

Most people are eventually able to move through this process with the support of family and friends. But some people get stuck and they find themselves unable to complete the process. This is when the aid of a trained counselor or support group is recommended.

As you move through the grieving process,

it will be helpful for you to gather support from others,

to be patient with yourself,

to give yourself time and space to work
through the process,

to understand that each person's
journey is unique,

and to know that the pain will diminish over time.

Recognize Unhealthy Behaviors

Recognize Unhealthy Behaviors

Pregnancy loss can produce strong emotions that may change over time.

Denying, repressing, or pushing down these emotions may work for a while, but continued refusal to face these emotions can lead to unhealthy behaviors.

>Miscarriage can represent significant loss(es) in a person's life.

Identifying and acknowledging these losses is an important step toward healing.

On the other hand, minimizing or denying them and the grief they produce will not only impede the healing process, but may also lead to unhealthy behaviors.

>*Unhealthy behaviors that may have been present before the miscarriage are likely to continue or accelerate after the miscarriage.*

In the beginning, unhealthy behaviors may be used as protective measures to either cope with or mask painful emotions, or to deny grief and loss. If the behaviors are repeatedly used, they may begin to consume or control your life.

Unhealthy behaviors may be a daily occurrence, or they may occur periodically. Sometimes unhealthy behaviors are triggered by certain events, such as the anniversary of the miscarriage or the expected due date of the child.

>*Whether or not you think these behaviors are related to the miscarriage, extra assistance such as a 12-step program or group, spiritual assistance, or professional counseling is needed to regain your well-being.*

Unhealthy Behaviors

Examples of unhealthy behaviors are listed below. Even if you don't think you're participating in unhealthy behaviors, please take a moment to look over the list.

If you suspect you may be using some of these behaviors, please take the time to visit a website or make a phone call to determine if you need assistance.

Remember, you are not alone!

- Anger
- Anxiety
- Compulsive disorders
- Cutting/self-abuse
- Depression
- Eating disorders
- Difficulty getting close to children, your partner, friends
- Frozen emotions
- Gambling and overspending
- Mood swings
- Overworking
- Phobia
- Risky behaviors (risk taking)
- Self-medicating with alcohol and/or drugs
- Sexual dysfunction or sexual acting out
- Suicidal thoughts
- Unhealthy or abusive relationships
- Violence

A list of resources for addressing these behaviors can be found on the Miscarriage Hurts website: MiscarriageHurts.com/healing-pathways/unhealthy-behaviors.

Complicated Grief

There are times when people get stuck in their grief and find themselves unable to continue the process. Or they may find that grief has become the center of their lives.

> While it's important not to set a particular time frame for healing, you also don't want to allow yourself to remain stuck for too long.

If you've experienced any of these symptoms for more than a month, you may be developing complicated grief or some other psychological complication. To rule out these possibilities, consultation with a trained counselor is recommended.

Possible Signs of Complicated Grief
- Anxiety
- Dulled sense of feeling
- Fear or avoidance of children
- Fixating on your lost child or another child
- Flashbacks
- Nightmares
- Rage
- Difficulty sleeping
- Difficulty concentrating
- Inability to recall parts of the event

Begin Healing

Begin Healing

If you've told your story,

> built a support system,

> explored your emotions,

> identified and begun grieving your losses,

> and recognized any unhealthy behaviors,

> then you've made significant progress.

You've made the decision to be honest about your experience and the impact it's had on your life.

As you continue to move through the healing process,

> please keep in mind that healing doesn't mean you have it all together.

>> It means that you're taking purposeful steps to go through a process.

Over time you may experience other emotions. However, if that happens, you'll have the resources to draw upon to help you deal with them.

If you haven't done so already, it's time to make another decision:

> To let go of the pain.

Surprisingly, this isn't as easy as it sounds...

Sometimes we get used to the pain,

> sometimes we hang on to the pain,

>> and sometimes we're afraid to move on.

Letting go of the pain will mean very different things for different people.

> For some it will mean letting go of shame or guilt.

>> For others it will mean letting go of anger or blame.

>>> And for others it will mean creating a different vision for their future.

But one thing that it doesn't mean is letting go of the memory of – and love for – your child.

> *Please keep in mind that your loss is no less real once you decide to let go of the pain.*

On the contrary, the loss takes its place as a part of your unique history—no longer hidden or suppressed, but integrated into your past and contributing to who you are now and will continue to be in the future.

Memorializing Your Child

Many men and women – and their families – find that preserving the memory of their child in some manner helps them to grieve and begin healing.

There are many ways this can be done such as:

> naming your child,*

> writing a letter to your child,

> putting together a scrapbook, photo album, or memories box,

> planning a ceremony,

> planting a tree,

> buying a piece of jewelry.

The important thing is to proceed how you think is best and feels most natural.

When you're ready, we invite you to acknowledge your pain and your decision to let go of it.

I've decided to let go of my pain.

I've decided to continue the process of healing.

_____

Name   Date

This doesn't signify that healing is concluded, it simply signifies your willingness to move forward in the journey.

For now,

      please journey at your own pace,

         know that you are not alone,

            and remember to hang on to hope.

Wishing you peace,

Michaelene and *Carol*

*We invite you to add your child's name to the memorial wall on MiscarriageHurts.com.

Use this space to continue your healing journey.

Additional Resources

MiscarriageHurts.com

Safe Place App

LifePerspectives.com

Links to other resources including sympathy cards
and memorial items can be found at LifePerspectives.com